THE
DRESS I'LL WEAR
TO THE PARTY

by **Shirley Neitzel**

pictures by
Nancy Winslow Parker

Greenwillow Books, New York

For Christine,
whose first word
was "pretty"

Black pen, watercolor paints, and
colored pencils were used
for the full-color art.
The text type is Seagull.

Text copyright © 1992
by Shirley Neitzel
Illustrations copyright © 1992
by Nancy Winslow Parker

Printed in Singapore by
Tien Wah Press
First Edition
10 9 8 7 6 5 4 3 2 1

Library of Congress
Cataloging-in-Publication Data
Neitzel, Shirley.
    The dress I'll wear to the party
by Shirley Neitzel ;
pictures by Nancy Winslow Parker.
      p.   cm.
    Summary:
In cumulative verses and
rebuses a girl describes
how she is dressing
up in her mother's
party things.
    ISBN 0-688-09959-9.
    ISBN 0-688-09960-2 (lib. bdg.)
    [1. Clothing and dress—Fiction.
2. Rebuses.
3. Stories in rhyme.]
I. Parker, Nancy Winslow, ill.
II. Title.
PZ8.3.N34Dr   1992
[E]—dc20
91-30906   CIP   AC

This is the dress I'll wear to the party.

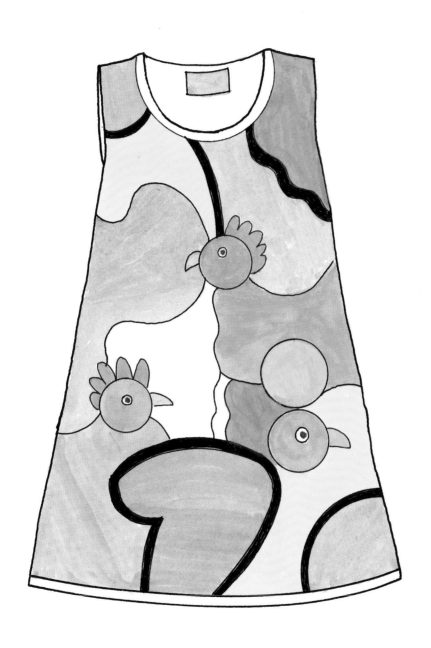

These are the shoes, shiny and black,

that peek from the hem of the

I'll wear to the party.

These are the buttons that fasten in back,

that match the  shiny and black,

that peek from the hem of the

I'll wear to the party.

This is the ribbon I pin in my hair,

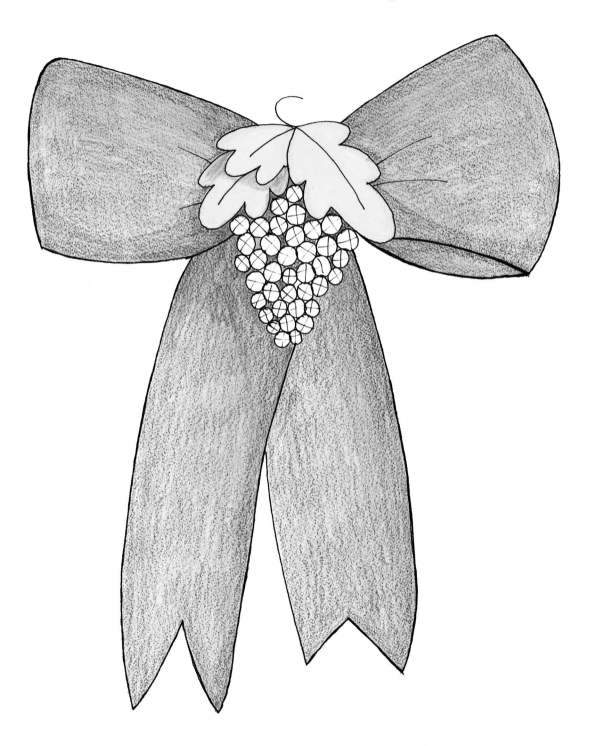

that touches the that fasten in back,

that match the shiny and black,

that peek from the hem of the

I'll wear to the party.

This is the perfume that scents the air,

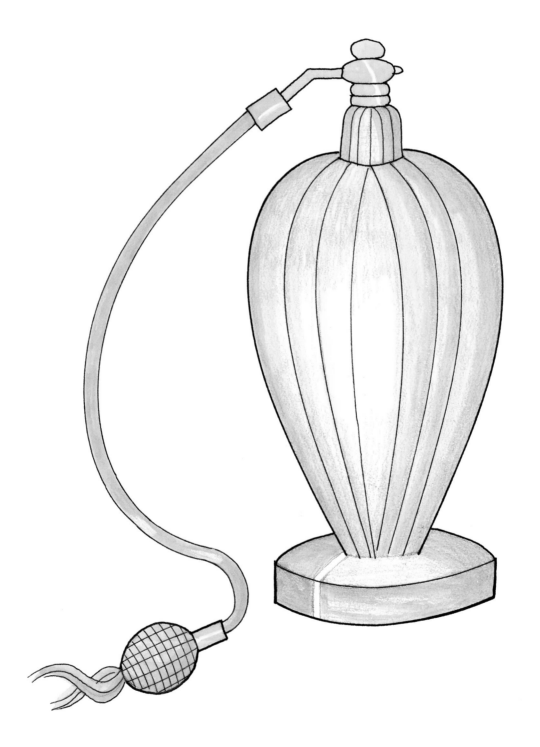

as I toss the  I pin in my hair,

that touches the that fasten in back,

that match the shiny and black,

that peek from the hem of the

I'll wear to the party.

These are the pearls I wear near my face,

when I spray the that scents the air,

as I toss the I pin in my hair,

that touches the that fasten in back,

that match the shiny and black,

that peek from the hem of the

I'll wear to the party.

This is the handkerchief, edged in lace,

that polishes the 🔵 I wear near my face,

when I spray the 🧴 that scents the air,

as I toss the 🎀 I pin in my hair,

that touches the ⚫ that fasten in back,

that match the 👠 shiny and black,

that peek from the hem of the 👗

I'll wear to the party.

This is the purse with the velvet band,

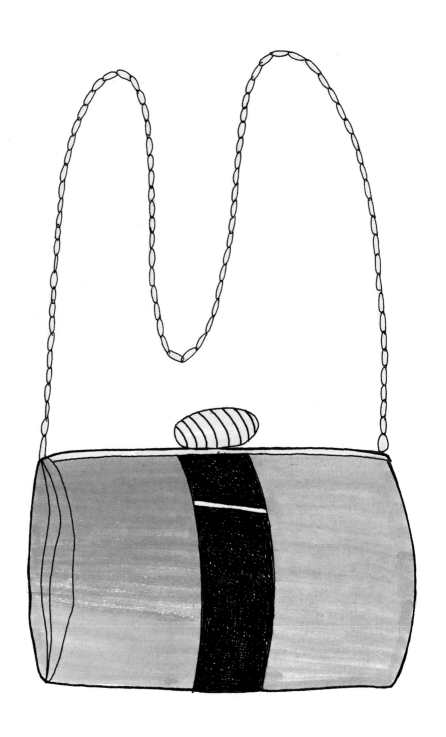

where I tuck the edged in lace,

that polishes the I wear near my face,

when I spray the that scents the air,

as I toss the I pin in my hair,

that touches the that fasten in back,

that match the shiny and black,

that peek from the hem of the

I'll wear to the party.

These are the rings I slip on my hand,

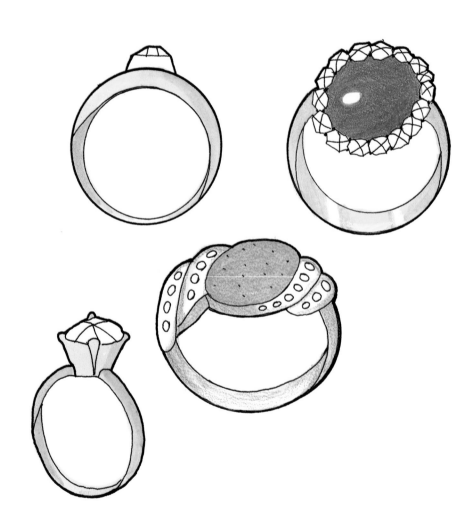

that carries the ▢ with the velvet band,

where I tuck the ▢ edged in lace,

that polishes the ▢ I wear near my face,

when I spray the ▢ that scents the air,

as I toss the ▢ I pin in my hair,

that touches the ▢ that fasten in back,

that match the ▢ shiny and black,

that peek from the hem of the ▢

I'll wear to the party.

These are the diamonds I clip on each ear,

that shine like the 💍 I slip on my hand,

that carries the 👜 with the velvet band,

where I tuck the 🧻 edged in lace,

that polishes the 📿 I wear near my face,

when I spray the 🧴 that scents the air,

as I toss the 🎀 I pin in my hair,

that touches the ⚫ that fasten in back,

that match the 👠 shiny and black,

that peek from the hem of the 👗

I'll wear to the party.

This is my mother who said, "Oh, dear!,"

then reached for the diamonds I'd clipped
on each ear,

and took the rings I'd slipped on my hand,
and unclasped the purse with the velvet band,

and pulled out the handkerchief edged in lace,
and wiped the pearls I'd worn near my face,
that glistened with perfume
that scented the air,

and undid the ribbon I'd pinned in my hair,

and opened the buttons that fastened in back,

and took off the shoes, shiny and black.

"You may not wear my things to the party!"

So...

this is the dress I'll wear to the party.

THE OUTCAST: RED MESA

LUKE CYPHER

WHEELER PUBLISHING
A part of Gale, Cengage Learning

GALE
CENGAGE Learning˙

Detroit • New York • San Francisco • New Haven, Conn • Waterville, Maine • London